DIVORCE AND REMARRIAGE IN THE BIBLE

A BEKY Book ©

Robin Gould, D.R.E., LMFT

Copyright © Robin Gould, 2016

Printed in the United States of America

Without limiting the rights under copyright reserved above, no part of this publication may be reproduced, stored in, or introduced into a retrieval system, or transmitted, in any form, or by any means (electronic, mechanical, photocopying, recording, or otherwise), without the prior written permission of the copyright owner.

Cover design by Rubel Photography, Mt. Juliet, TN

Screenshots courtesy of Bible Hub

This booklet is a BEKY Book publication: Books Encouraging the Kingdom of Yeshua. www.bekybooks.com

ISBN-13: 9780996183963

DEDICATION

This book is dedicated to those who have walked in pain and bondage to what we have been told, rather than walking in the freedom of what He has told us.

CONTENTS

	Glossary	7
	Preface	9
	Introduction	11
1	Ancient Codes and Covenant	13
2	Questions of Divorce and Remarriage	21
3	Lost and Found in Translation	27
4	Context, Context, Context!	43
5	Conclusion	57
	Study Review Questions	59
	Appendices	61
	References	71
	About the Author	73
	Acknowledgements	75

GLOSSARY

Aphorism - a statement of truth or opinion expressed in a summarizing and clever way. Its use is often applied to principles. (Example; "All's well that ends well.")

Bound - to be betrothed or to be married.

Canaan - a Semitic speaking region in the Ancient Near East during the late 2nd millennium that is now known as Israel.

Divorce - to legally dissolve a marriage in writing.

Hammurabi - the former King of Babylon (AKA: Nimrod) during 2400 BCE and 2100 BCE.

Hedonistic - engaged in the pursuit of pleasure, sensually self-indulgent, where the individual believes that pleasure is the primary good.

Fault covenant - a covenant with terms that can be annulled upon violation of those terms.

Faultless covenant - a covenant with no terms set forth that is kept by the covenant initiator on behalf of his or her word.

Put Away - to send one's spouse away without a legal divorce writ.

Fornication - an unlawful sexual union, forbidden by the laws of God.

Law of the Husband - a Torah marital law that states that remarriage to a former husband is forbidden by an ex-wife who later married someone else.

Loosed - to be released from the bonds of marriage due to a legal divorce or death of the spouse.

Gnosticism - the belief that matter, including the human body, is evil and that God has a far removed role from interacting with humanity, so salvation is driven by knowledge.

Misogyny - hatred, disrespect, and distrust of women; seeing women as inferior to men and thus treated as second class citizens.

Platonic anthropology - a philosophy that views unity in the human elements and their environment as a means to gain better understanding of values, responses, and outcomes in life.

Writ of divorce - written, legal document of the dissolution of a marriage.

PREFACE

This book was written to be an educational tool, but also as a salve. The issue of divorce and remarriage has wounded people for millennia, from young children to the elderly. Inaccurate divorce theology has brutally crumbled the opportunities God provided for healing, restoration, and freedom. Well-meaning pastors struggle with the inner conflict of obeying the Scriptures *or* being inclusive to the many remarried people genuinely seeking a stable church home and Godly community to help rebuild their lives. These ministers have gone to bed for far too many nights with the burning question of how it could be God's will to deprive wounded souls of needed fellowship. May this book settle this internal battle and inspire these good shepherds to open wide the door of invitation to these loving, God-fearing people.

I pray that this book will be a safe haven for those walking the lonely path of panic, fearing that they are in a state of adultery in a subsequent marriage. Those who have suffered in loveless, unstable marriages, succumbing to fractured trust and broken dreams, I am asking to come out of the shadows and into the light of His truth. May the Scriptures become armor against the naysayers who are more interested in what "they" have been saying than the actual words of Scripture, even the words of our Messiah Yeshua (Jesus). The liberty He has provided to abide in safe, loving marriages is built into His perfect Law governing the union between husband and wife. These laws of liberty are often obscured or misunderstood, so let's hear them now. It matters.

Christ's words in the Gospels can tear down walls of guilt and bring peace to wars fought within families who felt they were betraying God if they accepted the new spouse of their loved one. For the children of divorce carrying the shame of what is so often viewed as the sin rather than the solution to the sin, the simple words of this book offer comfort. To a child, words like "fault" and "no fault" mean nothing. What matters is that the foundations of their lives have been shaken apart, and the grace of the Father's Words ministered through His Son Yeshua should be just that, grace. If those children of divorce find that grace in the Word, then this booklet will achieve its purpose.

INTRODUCTION

The Bible says divorce and remarriage is not adultery. This statement might surprise you, for in much of the mainstream church, this statement is rejected. Many people who have remarried after divorce are suffering under the false accusation that their remarriages constitute "adultery." In many cases, the marriage is not seen as valid.

This teaching, that remarriage after divorce is adultery, emerged from a mistranslation of a word in Matthew 5:32, leading to a long-held, but incorrect assumption. Few people are exempt from the fallout of this issue. If you are not divorced yourself, you probably know of friends or family who have been divorced. You might be romantically interested in a divorced person. You might be divorced and remarried, but terrified that your marriage is an abomination to the One True God.

A pastor might feel forced to shun prospective church members because they divorced or are in remarriages. A marriage officiant might believe he is compromising a biblical principle by performing marital ceremonies for people who had previous marriages. Whatever connection with this issue one might have, this is one of the most common trials suffered by believers, and yet one of the least understood.

The outcome of scriptural error is pain, bondage, and shunning, as well as a misunderstanding of the unity between the Father and the Son. Thankfully, this is a problem with a solution: the truth. The truth pierces through the darkness created by this misunderstanding.

1

ANCIENT CODES AND COVENANT

The Code of Hammurabi (AKA: The Ancient Babylonian Law Code)

All proper study starts at the beginning. One should reach as far back as possible to get proper context and a good foundation. In this particular topic of marriage, divorce, and remarriage, there is historically proven information from which to break ground; namely the Code of Hammurabi (Hahm-oo-rahb-i). You may have read about this code in a high school world history class.

The reason it is important to compare the Biblical law to ancient Mesopotamian law is that it is one of the fundamental rules of Biblical interpretation. In his textbook on the rules of Biblical hermeneutics, Kaiser states:

> "Recognize the significance of the biblical language for proper interpretation... accustom yourself to the notion that there is a linguistic and <u>cultural distance</u> that separates us from the biblical text. While this distance should not be exaggerated, beware of reading into the Bible ideas that can be supported only from the English translation." (Kaiser, 1994, p. 63)

> "Do place priority on the attested and <u>contemporary usage of words</u>...writers depend on <u>the way language is actually used in their time</u>." (Kaiser, p. 64)

Because this ancient Code chronicles the cultural, legal, political, social and economic mindset of the time and place in which the Scriptures were given to Israel, it is a valuable resource to contrast a loving Father's instructions to His imperfect children with the ancient monarchal laws.

This code is the first manmade law code to be written and formally established. The emphasis here is on "manmade," not God-made. Hammurabi's Code is the known law of the Mesopotamian region in the early "Old Testament" (Tanakh) era. Created by "The King of Babylon" (AKA: Nimrod, as mentioned in the book of *Jasher*), this code was administered between 2400 BCE and 2100 BCE, which was during the time of Noah. This law code often deviates from God's eternal law (Torah) as written by Moses, but it records the norm of the land during that time and its legacy in later Near Eastern civil codes.

Similarly, when we compare modern law codes to the Bible, there are differences and similarities. The situation in ancient Mesopotamia/Canaan was no different. In fact, in atheist apologetics, the accusation is that the Torah copies the Code of Hammurabi since some of it is so similar to the Code, even in wording. Since God's law predates all other law, the believer will argue that the Code copied the Torah.

The Scriptures, however, present sound evidence that even before the Torah was given to Moses at Mt. Sinai, people in the ancient Near and Middle East observed many of those laws. For instance, Noah knew the difference between clean and unclean animals, and Rachel knew the laws of *niddah* (menstruation).

While the Torah was not written down until it was given to Moses on Mt Sinai, it was still the first law of all laws. Abraham knew God's laws:

> Because that Abraham obeyed my voice,
> and kept my charge, my commandments,
> my statutes, and my laws. (Genesis 26:5 KJV)

The Hebrews had forgotten God's law in their enslavement in Egypt, thus requiring significant correction. They had to be taught where the God of Israel, Egyptian custom (see Appendix A), and Hammurabi disagreed on protocol and practice, and the Father was faithful to do just that for His beloved Israel.

In Hammurabi's Babylonian Law Code, divorce was permitted in specified circumstances with the outcomes favoring the "innocent" party. Divorce was verbally rendered by the husband against a wife he considered guilty of breaking the marital contract for a variety of reasons. After being verbally divorced by her husband, the wife was sent away with nothing. The samples from the Code's divorce laws in Appendix B demonstrate how vulnerable women were to a divorce code that required no official certificate of divorce. Husbands could always dispute the grounds for divorce and delay a divorce at best, or neglect to pay her dowry settlement at worst.

As barbaric as that might sound, because Americans are governed by a legal system requiring more legwork to divorce than it takes to marry, this was the normative practice for what was the only developed region at that time. It was the standardized form of thought, and thus, very important to understand so that we may hear through the ears of those receiving the correction at that time.

It is a reasonable assumption that Adonai's (the God of Israel) correction was given against the standard of the day, *with the corrections being highlighted* rather than every detail being reiterated. Adonai knew the prevailing laws of marriage and divorce, and He taught in context with what He knew they knew. This people-group receiving the Torah from Moses knew their contemporary law code, but they had forgotten Adonai's law. Hammurabi's Code drew from Adonai's code, but with differences of laws, or parts of laws added or removed. The King of Babylon had his personal, self-serving twist since he considered himself the ultimate master to be served. Since Adonai is the ultimate Master, and Hammurabi's Code deviated from His perfect law, the correction was made clear by Adonai when He gave Moses the Law of the Torah.

This survey of Near Eastern ancient covenant practices supplies knowledge of what was considered the norm of the day, opening the understanding of what the people would have already understood to be the unchallenged status quo of Mesopotamian society's cultural and legal reality of contracts/covenants.

Contracts and Covenants

First, the average Bible student usually has not examined and compared the features and structure of the various Torah covenants. Believers in Yeshua (Jesus) wish to live biblically; therefore, they learn to distinguish between conditional and unconditional covenants because these are very important covenant structures found in the Bible.

Briefly, Adonai makes two kinds of covenants with mankind.

They are:

1. Fault covenants (conditional)
2. Faultless covenants (unconditional)

A conditional contract or covenant is one that stipulates conditions to which both parties are accountable. In the case of violation by one of the parties, the damaged party has the right to annul the contract. Categorically, marital contracts are conditional contracts, as both parties accept terms. This was the standard understanding and practice in the Ancient Near East. The Code of Hammurabi and the instruction of Adonai are undistinguishable on this point (see Appendix B for examples of "fault"). Some people consider marriage covenants unconditional because they have never learned about covenants from a biblical perspective, but from an emotional perspective.

Fault Covenants

Fault covenants are contracts where both parties making the covenant participate in a procedure of acceptance of terms and penalties. If one of the parties is at fault and violates the terms of the covenant, the covenant is void. The party at fault then endures the established penalty.

Here is an example of a fault covenant. A grandfather is delighted at the birth of his first grandchild. As a provision for the child, the grandfather promises to pay for the child's college education provided that the child has no criminal record or illegal activity. If the child reaches college age and has remained free from legal problems, the contract is invoked and the payment must be rendered. If, however, the child reaches college age and has been penalized for a crime such as shoplifting or destruction of personal property, the fault clause is invoked, and payment is not rendered. Contractually, there is a behavioral component to this payment, and if the conditions are not met, the contract of payment for the college education is void.

Faultless Covenants

Faultless covenants are covenants where one party makes a vow, as an individual, to abide by the terms set forth, regardless of the second party's actions. In these covenants, there are no terms set except those promised by the carrier of the responsibilities of the covenant, and there is no established penalty. The second party is the beneficiary of the outcome of the responsible first party keeping the vow. These contracts are usually self-administered by a stronger party to a weaker party as a provisional effort.

Using the first example, if the grandfather were to make a faultless covenant with the grandchild, the stipulation would be that the grandfather would pay for the college education, period. There is no behavioral component. The grandfather is simply obligated to pay for the child's college education based on his promise to do so. Even if the child engaged in illegal activity, even if he had spent time in juvenile detention, the contract is still enforceable based on the contractual promise the grandfather made. The contract is unconditional on the part of the recipient of the provision, but it is binding on the giver.

Here is a biblical example of a faultless covenant.

> This is the sign of the covenant which I am making between Me and you and every living creature that is with you, for all successive generations; I set My bow in the cloud, and it shall be for a sign of a covenant between Me and the earth. (Genesis 9:12-13)

This is another example that more dramatically highlights the faultless covenant:

> And it came to pass, that when the sun went down, and it was dark, behold a smoking furnace, and a burning lamp that passed between those pieces... (Genesis 15:17)

In this blood covenant, which was a procedure common to Near Eastern practices, the land of Israel was promised to Abraham's descendants. However, Abraham was put in a deep sleep while the capital punishment vow was sealed with the passing of the smoking furnace and flaming torch. This signaled that if the covenant was broken, the death penalty would be the burden of the One who passed through the pieces regardless of the actions of the descendants of Abraham. It was faultless for Abraham and his descendants, but it had a fault burden on what passed through the pieces, which this writer believes is YHWH (Jehovah) and Yeshua, i.e., the smoking furnace and the lamp (Rev. 21:23) that was lit off that furnace respectively.

A marital covenant from a biblical standpoint is not a faultless covenant. The Western view of marital covenants is varied, whereas in the Ancient Near East, it was commonly known that marital contracts were always fault contracts designed to accomplish several vital goals for individuals and communities to thrive. A marriage is an agreement entered into by two participating parties, setting forth terms, and making vows to keep those terms.

The Hebrews call this agreement a *Ketubah*. In Hebrew this means "written thing." It is an arrangement with conditions that provide an option of release if the conditions are abandoned by one party. Therefore, divorce, which is the dissolution of the marital union due to a violation of the marital contract, is indeed lawful. This was normative thinking in this region from the time of Noah (and earlier) until the time the Torah was given to Moses on Mt. Sinai.

Contrast the ancient practice with current perspectives lacking respect for God's law. Western law codes lack the unification of one law for all. In Western society there are various religious systems that view the marriage vows as unconditional. In other words, both parties make vows and promise to remain in the union even if the other party abandons the terms of the contract. Interestingly, secular marital unions are often viewed from a more biblical lens: when one of the parties abandons the terms of the contract, it is generally not taboo to seek release from the broken covenant in the form of divorce.

For example:

> In Adonai's marriage to Israel at Mt. Sinai, the bride vowed to walk in His ways and accept His authority (see Ex. 19:3-8).

> Adonai, for His part, vowed to bestow on them the birthright and the Kingdom, honor and protection (see Gen. 12:1-3).

Israel desecrated this contract, breaking her vows and rejecting many opportunities of repentance. As a result, her Husband divorced her (in writing) and sent her out of His house (Jer. 3:8; Hosea 2:2). When the Northern Kingdom split from the house of Judah, they (the Northern Kingdom) continuously engaged in idol worship that included covenantal rituals for other gods involving blood, trees, sacrifice, self-mutilation, and sexual acts. The Northern Kingdom of Israel gave herself intimately to foreign gods. Loyalty and faith were bestowed to idols, gods that were not gods.

2

QUESTIONS OF DIVORCE AND REMARRIAGE

Is Divorce a Sin?

Because Adonai initiated a divorce, we know that divorce itself is not a sin. Rather, divorce is the outcome of sin; sin is defined in the Bible as transgression of the commandments (see 1 John 3:4). Divorce is the resolution of the sin problem when trust has been irrevocably fractured and the marital union no longer functions in its intended design.

Israel broke the covenant, so Adonai divorced them. The divorce is legal and binding. When one or both parties refuse to participate constructively in the marriage, the union no longer serves its purpose. Marriage was created to be a tool for people to live better lives, to raise Godly seed, to walk in the example of the Creator, and to be a light to unbelievers.

People were not created to be tools for marriage where they submit to an unconditional contract of nebulous terms, constantly embroiled in a life that is actually an obstacle to achieving these wonderful things. *That line of thinking actually sets up marriage to be an idol we serve.*

What is Adonai's law on divorce and remarriage from His

own mouth? His clear instruction on divorce and remarriage plainly is specified:

> When a man hath taken a wife, and married her, and it come to pass that she finds no favour in his eyes, because he hath found some uncleanness in her: then let him write her a bill of divorcement, and give it in her hand, and send her out of his house. And when she is departed out of his house, she may go and be another man's wife. And if the latter husband hate her, and write her a bill of divorcement, and giveth it in her hand, and sendeth her out of his house; or if the latter husband die, which took her to be his wife; her former husband, which sent her away, may not take her again to be his wife, after that she is defiled; for that is abomination before the LORD: and thou shalt not cause the land to sin, which the LORD thy God giveth thee for an inheritance. (Deuteronomy 24:1-4 KJV)

Special Circumstances

Are there circumstances where marriage is not dissolvable? Yes. In certain conditions that are specified in Deuteronomy 22:13-30, God does not allow the violating spouse to dissolve the marriage covenant. Divorce was permitted **except when circumstances put women at a disadvantage**. In these cases, as a provisionary measure for the wellbeing of women, God withheld the prospect of divorce.

The following are the two circumstances where divorce is not permitted:

1. When the husband falsely claimed that his new wife was not a virgin "the husband brought a bad name upon her," "...He cannot divorce her all his days" (Deuteronomy 22:19 NIV)

2. When a man had sex with a virgin single woman. He must

pay support money (the dowry of a bride) to her family, and by having sex with her he had ostensibly taken her as his wife and could never divorce her. (Deuteronomy 22:29 NIV)

The legality of the second marriage was at her father's discretion. If he so desired, the marriage would be annulled, and father and daughter would keep the dowry (see Exodus 22:16). A bride's dowry in the Ancient Near East was always considered the property of the bride. The dowry was a safety net for the wife in the case of her being divorced or widowed, as it was stored for her and returned if needed (see Appendix B).

Those are the only two Scriptural cases where the covenant of marriage was not permitted to be dissolved; however, the wife was allowed to divorce her husband in these cases. A lawful divorce was always permissible when the marriage covenant was dishonored except in these cases where limits were placed on the man to protect women.

Let's review what Adonai Himself says about divorce and remarriage before moving on to further points.

> When a man hath taken a wife, and
> married her, and it come to pass that she
> finds no favour in his eyes, because he hath
> found some uncleanness in her: then let him
> write her a bill of divorcement, and give it
> in her hand, and send her out of his house.
> (Deut. 24:1 KJV)

And then must she remain single? Look again at verse 2:

> And when she is departed out of his house,
> she may go and be another man's wife.
> (Deut. 24:2)

Remarriage is not prohibited.

"Just grounds" for a Divorce

There is no provision for a "faultless divorce," so there must be a cause for divorce. Since no details are provided in the biblical text about what this causation for divorce is, one can deduce that the union was in some way compromised and no longer serving its intended purpose. Why were details not provided for such a vital matter?

Not knowing the answer to this question has led some who are uninformed of the common law of the Ancient Near East to "fill in the blanks" with their own interpretations of what these offenses are. Some teachers instruct that "finding uncleanness in her" or "finding no favor in his eyes" means adultery, and that divorce is only lawful in case of adultery. It's beneficial to point out here that **the established penalty for adultery is death, not divorce.**

Some assert divorce is only permissible if the husband discovers that his wife had sexual relations with someone prior to their marriage and concealed this act from him. However, again, this also calls for the death penalty (see Deut. 22:13-21). Acceptable reasons for divorce referred to in Deuteronomy 24 must be something else.

Since the grounds are not itemized, it would seem that the common law required no adjusting here. This is where the Code of Hammurabi is useful, for it states constituted acceptable grounds for divorce. Adonai was speaking to people who had a context of law already based on the undisputed common law of a unified society. Right or wrong, they were unified in one, single, known law of that day. Proper biblical interpretation (hermeneutics) demands that the reader question what the understanding was of the people to whom a document was written at that time, not the understanding in modern American culture.

According to the law that the people knew at that time, grounds for both genders were specified: cruelty, slander, squandering family assets, acquiring frivolous debts, as well as any other specific contract violation. Additional grounds for *just the wife* included lack of physical support and refusal of conjugal relations, which compares equally with Exodus 21:10-11.

Since no more details are clarified by Adonai on such an important matter, one can conclude that grounds for divorce in the common law were acceptable to Him, and were probably the grounds He taught to Adam, and Adam taught to Noah (remember the long life spans of these early people).

However, there is one big difference in Adonai's instruction on divorce from the Code of Hammurabi, and He makes His point very clear. The divorce **procedure** differs very significantly. The Code of Hammurabi allows the man to divorce his wife verbally. Adonai's instruction demands a written document be given to the wife. This is called "the writ," or "letter," or "bill of divorcement." Hammurabi's divorces were purely verbal. Adonai mandates a writ. Why?

Fairness for the woman is protected by the mandate of a written letter of divorcement. This is her proof that her former husband no longer has any spousal rights to her. It is also her written authorization to remarry. Adonai allows her to remarry once she has those divorce papers (refer to Deuteronomy 24:2). Remarriage without those divorce papers would be committing adultery, so that written document is very important indeed.

This is why Adonai seems redundant on the point that the husband is to "give it to her in her hand." This was a crucial part of her freedom to find security elsewhere. The Ancient Near East was not a "community college for single moms" society, nor were there many career options outside of domestic life. Women were limited in their job opportunities to positions of servitude or prostitution, so Adonai, in His great love and protection of women, safeguarded her position of spiritual and physical safety.

3

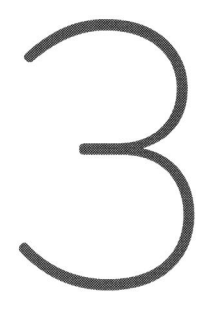

LOST AND FOUND IN TRANSLATION

With a good foundational knowledge of Ancient Near Eastern marriage laws, as well as how they were similar to and different from the Torah, take a look at some biblical terms regarding marriage and divorce. Correctly dividing the Word of truth reveals perfect consistency from the first page to the last.

The three main verbs describing aspects of marital action in the *Tanakh* (Old Testament) and New Testament are:

MARRY | PUT AWAY | DIVORCE

Adjectives to describe the statuses of the marital union as a result of these actions are BOUND and LOOSED.

Since "marry" is obvious from the Torah texts, let's focus on the other words. Some teachers and translators, unfamiliar with the Hebrew and Greek words for DIVORCE and PUT AWAY, use these words interchangeably. This leads to translation errors because "put away" does not mean "divorce."

Comparison of these words in the Old Testament

Put away

The term "put away" generally comes from the Hebrew words **shalach** ("to send away") or **garash** ("to drive away"). The words differ only in intensity. In reference to a husband and wife, it refers to the act of separation, where a man sends his wife out of the house.

Divorce

The term "divorce" is from the Hebrew word **kerithuth**. This word refers to the procedure by which the marriage relationship is lawfully terminated. It is used only four times in the Old Testament, and each time it is used in the full phrase, "bill of divorcement." (Deut. 24:1,3; Isaiah 50:1; Jer. 3:8)

Comparison of these words in the New Testament

Put away

Apoluo is the Greek word for "separate without divorce papers" to send away without writing. This is merely the physical separation of the union. This accompanies the act of divorcement but is not itself the divorce.

Divorce

The Greek word **Apostasion** for "divorce" comes from **Apo**, meaning "away from;" and **stasis**, meaning "standing, established (by law)" referring in this case to the written marriage contract. The word **apostasion** signifies more than a mere separation, or "putting away." It is the lawful disestablishment of the marriage contract, accomplished by the written bill of divorcement.

Marital statuses as a result of the previous marital actions

Bound
- Married or
- Betrothed, pledged

<u>Loosed</u>
Released from the marital union through
- The death of a spouse *or*
- A lawful, written divorce of procedure

Correct translations are critical. There are those who teach that a legal, written divorce is unlawful in the eyes of Adonai, and that divorce is only viewed by Him as a separation. From this perspective, any remarriage would be adultery against the "separated" spouse. This perspective competes with Adonai's instruction on divorce and remarriage.

This isn't logical even within the mainstream argument that adultery is the only out-clause for divorce and that the person who remarried is in a constant state of adultery. Why? If he or she is committing adultery in the new marriage, doesn't that itself create the grounds for divorce if adultery is that requirement? Do you see how that makes no sense?

Adonai's instruction mandates that a written divorce (kerithuth) *always* follow the putting away (shalach or garash) of a wife because without that specific, written document, simply putting away a wife does not establish a lawful divorce. Without an actual writ that she can hold in her hand, the woman is still legally considered a wife and is not eligible for remarriage.

If the husband fails to give her a letter of divorcement, he is guilty of neglecting to release her to acquire the provisional support of another husband, and he is liable for her adultery as much as she is.

Examples:

> This is what the LORD says: 'Where is your mother's *certificate of divorce with which I sent her away?* Or to which of my creditors did I sell you? Because of your sins you were sold; because of your transgressions your mother was sent away.' (Isaiah 50:1 NIV) and her second husband dislikes her and writes her a *certificate of divorce, gives it*

> to her and sends her from his house, or if he dies. (Deut. 24:3 NIV)

> And I saw that for all the adulteries of faithless Israel, I had sent her away and given her a writ of divorce, yet her treacherous sister Judah did not fear; but she went and was a harlot also. Because of the lightness of her harlotry, she polluted the land and committed adultery with stones and trees.... (Jer. 3:8-9 NASB)

The two terms "put away" and "divorce" are not one and the same. These actions always were to be applied together, but they do not mean the same thing at all. The understanding of each of these terms and their differences is imperative in order to comprehend Yeshua's words in Matthew 5:32.

Did Yeshua Ban Divorce and Remarriage?

> The Pharisees, attempting to trick Him, asked Jesus; 'Is it lawful to put away (*apoluo*) one's wife?' (Mark 10:2-9 KJV 2000)

Yeshua responded by asking them what Moses had said. In other words, He directed them right to the Torah where that instruction is found. Please note, He was not being asked if men could **divorce** their wives, but if they could simply "**put them away**" without the letter of divorce (see Appendix C).

When Yeshua asked what the Torah states about divorce, the Pharisees correctly answered that Moses had commanded them to write a bill of divorcement **and** to put her away. It was clear to them what the Torah said, but they were testing Yeshua to see if He would deviate from the Torah and justify their behavior of only putting their wives away and not following through with the actual written divorce.

By failing to put the certificate of divorce in the wife's hand, a husband could

1. Avoid paying the dowry, or ketubah settlement, which would be a source of financial support for the divorced wife until her remarriage.
2. Continue to derive and manage any profits he had made from her dowry. Although he was not permitted to squander her original dowry's value, he was entitled to the profits from its investment.

These antics are not so different from present-day divorce settlement disputes, and using the finalization of the divorce as leverage to benefit financially is not a new trick! In fact, God's Torah corrected an abuse with which the ancient Hebrews would have been familiar from their Egyptian captivity:

> But it seems clear that, until the husband has returned his wife's dowry and paid her the fine, or until she has accepted it, the husband remained liable for supporting her, even if they were no longer living together. Some (ex-)husbands, then as now, tried to avoid supporting their (ex-) wives. (Johnson, 2004)

Even within First Century Judaism, hard-hearted men devised ways to avoid the very Egyptian abuse that the Torah was designed to correct (see Appendix A).

Yeshua gives the reason that divorce is allowed. "For the hardness of your heart He wrote you this precept." He declared that divorce was not what marital unions were designed to accomplish when marriage was created in the Garden, but that it was added to accommodate free will. Yeshua is teaching that divorce is grievous, but because men's hearts can be hard, it is necessary that an acceptable and lawful method be in place for managing marriage contracts that had been violated.

As for the creation of laws in general, for example, Adonai established the death penalty as the method to manage first-degree murder offenses. Adonai created us to love

Him and to love others, but due to the hardness of some men's hearts, there had to be a lawful method in place to deter and manage murder. Having to enact any laws at all is only due to the hardness of men's hearts, (1Timothy 1:9) from murder, to friendship, to divorce. If all men were perfect, there would be no need for instructions. Marital law, including the provision for divorce, is no different from any other law. So long as there are imperfect men on the earth, there must be instructions to govern behavior.

Adonai did not create a contractual institution where an innocent party is held to the terms of the contract that the other party violates. The marital agreement with its terms is a conditional contract. Yeshua's declaration about the hardness of men's hearts should not be interpreted to mean that there is something wrong with *Adonai's law*, but rather there is something wrong with *some people*. He isn't suggesting that divorce itself is a sin, but it was added to be the solution for the sin...which is defined here as having a hard heart toward one's spouse. The sin was the hard heart, not the divorce.

Yeshua is not correcting His Father's law. He is correcting the Pharisees' interpretation and application of His Father's law. The Holy One of Israel needs no correction. The religious leaders of the day who were dealing with women treacherously needed correction, just as family courts today are in place to correct treacherous spouses in divorce cases. Remember, Adonai is the CREATOR. He is never backed into corners or forced to go against His own character to make decisions and laws. Adonai does not lead His people into bondage with His instructions. His instructions deliver us from bondage!

Did Yeshua Ban Remarriage after Divorce?

Matthew 5:31-32 is the passage sometimes used to prove that any remarriage after divorce is adultery. Here is the translation found in the King James translation:

> It hath been said, 'Whosoever shall put away his wife, let him give her a writing

of divorcement; but I say unto you, that whosoever shall put away his wife, saving for the cause of fornication, causeth her to commit adultery; and whosoever shall marry her that is divorced committeth adultery.'

The conclusion that a man who marries a divorced woman commits adultery is drawn from the translation of the Greek scripture in verse 32:

...whosoever shall marry her that is divorced committeth adultery. (KJV)

This statement *would appear* to state emphatically that ALL remarriage after divorce is adultery, and that no divorce is binding since the divorced woman can never be considered free for marriage.

Let's compare:

Adonai
"After she is divorced, she may go and be another man's wife." (Deut. 24)

Yeshua
"Whomever marries a divorced woman commits adultery." (Matt. 5:32)

If this translation was accurate, what is implied is that the Word of Adonai says that a woman may remarry after a divorce, but that it is a sin to marry a divorced woman. This is not a scholarly or even a logical conclusion.

First, it pits the Messiah's words against the Father's words. Second, it suggests that the Father's words change. It also puts one back into that circus of thought that on the one hand, *unless adultery occurred, the original marriage is still binding* but on the other hand, *the divorced person is committing adultery in her new marriage, but the previous marriage is still binding.*

With such reasoning, even if a husband is beating or mentally abusing his wife, harming his children, has left the faith, or taken up a life of drugs and gambling, any divorce outside of adultery would be considered a sin. Is that in the nature or character of Yeshua? Does this seem logical considering the intended function and design of marriage? Is this Yeshua vs. Adonai, or is it proper translation vs improper translation?

The passage in question is a part of Yeshua's Sermon on the Mount, which is a commentary on some Torah instructions that He saw misapplied. In verses 17-19 of that same chapter, Yeshua ardently disclaimed the idea that He was trying destroy or undermine the Torah instruction. Further, He positively condemned those who would relax even the least commandment and teach others to do so. From this alone, it should be clear that Yeshua did not abolish or alter Adonai's instructions on divorce and remarriage.

Here is the full context for His words in verses 31 and 32 (bracket mine):

> Do not think that I have come to abolish the Law or the Prophets; I have not come to abolish them but to fulfill [fully teach] them. For truly I tell you, until heaven and earth disappear, not the smallest letter, not the least stroke of a pen, will by any means disappear from the Law until everything is accomplished. Therefore anyone who sets aside one of the least of these commands and teaches others accordingly will be called least in the kingdom of heaven, but whoever practices and teaches these commands will be called great in the kingdom of heaven. For I tell you that unless your righteousness surpasses that of the Pharisees and the teachers of the law, you will certainly not enter the kingdom of heaven. (Matt. 5: 17-20 NIV)

Yeshua teaches that his disciples' righteousness must *surpass* that of the scribes and Pharisees, *not abandon it* - that would be the opposite!

He mentions the following Torah commandments:

1. Thou shalt not kill (vs. 21-26)
2. Thou shalt not commit adultery (vs 27-32)
3. Thou shalt not bear false witness (vs 33-37)
4. An eye for an eye (vs 38-42)
5. Thou shalt love thy neighbor as thyself (vs 43-48)

Yeshua is reminding the Pharisees to apply these instructions in Spirit and in Truth, not instructing them to put away the practical application of it when they rendered spiritual advice to troubled marriages. The husbands who were abusing the Torah and their wives were in error, not the Torah! What is more likely, that Yeshua was correcting the Creator, or that He was correcting its interpreters? Suggesting that Yeshua is correcting the Torah is a sincere misunderstanding of the goals and purpose of the Messiah and the true message of the Gospel.

In this teaching on the Mount, Yeshua did not modify the practical application of any law. He expanded the application to be generated from a heart of purity, not just technical obedience, or in this case, only partial obedience. In that same teaching, Yeshua discusses murder. He did NOT modify the practical application of the Law on murder when He said, "You have heard that it was said to those of old, 'You shall not murder, and whoever murders will be in danger of the judgment.' But I say to you that whoever is angry with his brother without a cause shall be in danger of the judgment." (NKJ) He expanded the understanding of the position of the heart when it came to hate, using the law of murder to frame it.

Yeshua also said "You have heard that it was said to those of old,'You shall not commit adultery.' But I say to you that whoever looks at a woman to lust for her has already committed adultery with her in his heart."(NKJ) Just because the man doesn't "look at a woman to lust for her" during the encounter does not make his actions justifiable. He was not saying to cease the action of obedience to these commandments as long as your "heart is pure." He is teaching them an *increase* in the observance by obeying in Spirit and Truth *from the heart*.

Some of the instructions of the Torah were being misapplied, and the true spirit of the Law had been lost through using the letter of the Torah as leverage to ignore the weightier matters of justice toward women. To use a "technicality" to deal with women treacherously is an abuse of the intent of the Torah. On a point where Yeshua is accused by the secular world of misogyny, He was actually asserting the rights of women upon those who would seek to neglect those God-given rights. How ironic. It's also ironic that the Messiah, touted by some as the opposing figure of grace to Adonai's lust for wrath, is the one prohibiting a woman to be forgiven of divorce, while Adonai allows her to be liberated and free.

Yeshua did not destroy or alter the Law in Matthew 5:31-32; he defines adultery according to the Torah instructions of divorce and remarriage. When He asks, "What did Moses say?", Yeshua is discussing Deuteronomy 24:1 and reminding questioners that Adonai commanded that the wife be provided with *a written bill of divorcement* for the divorce to be lawful, for in Deuteronomy 24:2, once a woman has such a decree, she is permitted to remarry.

So take another look at Matthew 5:31-32, inserting a few key words in the original Greek to obtain an accurate translation (see Appendix D).

> It hath been said, whosoever shall put away (*apoluo*) his wife, let him give her a writing of divorcement (*apostasion*). But I say unto you, that whosoever shall put away (*apoluo*) his wife, saving for the cause of fornication, causeth her to commit adultery: and whosoever shall marry her that is ~~divorced~~ (*apoluo*, Lit. "put away") committeth adultery. (Matthew 5:31-32)

Now read the accurate translation:

I say, whosoever shall put away (*apoluo*) his wife, let him give her a writing of divorcement (*apostasion*). But I say unto you, that whosoever shall put away (*apoluo*) his wife, saving for the cause of fornication, causeth her to commit adultery: and whosoever shall marry her that is put away (*apoluo*) committeth adultery. (Matt 5:31-32)

Side-by-Side Comparison

Mistranslated

It hath been said, 'Whosoever shall put away his wife, let him give her a writing of divorcement.' But I say unto you, that whosoever shall put away his wife, saving for the cause of fornication, causeth her to commit adultery: and whosoever shall marry her that is **divorced** committeth adultery.

Properly Translated

It hath been said, 'Whosoever shall put away his wife, let him give her a writing of divorcement.' But I say unto you, that whosoever shall put away his wife, saving for the cause of fornication, causeth her to commit adultery: and whosoever shall marry her that is **put away** committeth adultery.

To summarize Yeshua's statement:

> *The instruction demands a writ. If she does not have a writ, she commits adultery if she remarries without it.*

This summary is drawn from Yeshua's very specific wording. Parenthetical notes are understood based on the foundational Torah Law: "But I say to you that whoever **puts her away** (without a writ) causes her to commit adultery (if she has no writ but remarries regardless out of desperation)." As a result, he who sends her away without a writ shares responsibility of that sin with the wife he sent out. Any man who marries a woman who has been put away with no writ commits adultery as well because she is still legally married to another man.

Yeshua is reproving men who put away their wives only verbally as the Babylonian common law allowed instead of legally divorcing them as instructed by Adonai. Yeshua is not rebuking them for divorcing their wives. He is rebuking them for NOT divorcing them! This gross negligence of partial obedience makes the first husband liable for her adultery as well. Again, Yeshua was correcting this disgraceful treatment of women. He was not creating new laws, amending any established laws, or changing anything at all.

The written decree was testimony on behalf of the divorced woman so that her former spouse could never make a future claim of adultery against her, a method superior to Hammurabi's, in which a lack of witnesses to a verbal dismissal by the husband left the ex-wife with no proof of dissolution. The written decree commanded by the God of Israel was an extra step designed to protect a divorced woman from a malicious ex-husband, yet this very act of compassion toward women was sometimes twisted to abuse them in the First Century.

Yeshua repeats His point to His disciples in Mark 10:11-12:

Incorrect translation

When they were in the house again, the disciples asked Jesus about this. He answered, "Anyone who ~~divorces~~ his wife and marries another woman commits adultery against her. And if she ~~divorces~~ her husband and marries another man, she commits adultery." (Mark 10:11-12)

Correct translation

When they were in the house again, the disciples asked Jesus about this. He answered, "Anyone who <u>puts away</u> his wife and marries another woman commits adultery against her. And if she <u>separates from</u> her husband and marries another man, she commits adultery." (Mark 10:11-12)

This can be verified in the interlinear text. The very question that the scribes and Pharisees asked Yeshua was if it was lawful to put away one's wife. They were either testing Yeshua to catch Him altering Torah (which would discredit Him as the Messiah), or seeing whether He would condone simply dismissing a wife verbally without the second required step of giving her a writ. Yeshua answered by invoking Torah law, stating that they ALSO had to give her a writ of divorcement. He details the one case where divorce papers are not needed, which is in the case of fornication.

"Saving for the Cause of Fornication"

Many assume Yeshua's statement means that if a wife commits adultery, it is then and *only then* that the divorced woman could remarry, or even that this is the only lawful divorce, but notice that the cause mentioned is not adultery. The words "adultery" and "fornication" are both used in the same sentence, an important contextual clue.

In Galatians 5:19 and Mark 7:21, both the words "adultery" and "fornication" are used in the same verse. *They are different words with different meanings.* The Greek word for fornication is *pornia* while the word for adultery is *moicheia*.

What is intended by the word "fornication?" Why is it permissible, according to Yeshua, to "put away" (separate without a written divorce) your partner in the case of fornication? The most mentioned form of fornication in the Bible is prostitution, which is when a sexual relationship occurs between a man and a woman who is not married, often for compensation. The resolution for this relationship to regain Godly behavior would be to marry or to send the prostitute away.

Fornication also applies to other various forbidden sexual encounters. Those in Sodom and Gomorrah (Jude 7) who had given themselves over to "fornication" engaged in homosexuality, or "sodomy" (Gen. 19:4-8). Paul uses "fornication" to describe another forbidden act of sexual union, incest, first described in Leviticus 18:6-8.

Paul writes:

> It is reported commonly that there is fornication among you, and such fornication as is not so much as named among the gentiles, that one should have his father's wife. (1 Cor. 5:1 KJV)

Hebrews 12:16 describes Esau as a fornicator with no mention of him being with a prostitute anywhere in the bible. It is well established in Genesis 26:34 that Esau took forbidden women as his wives. He married Hittite women despite being expressly commanded not to, as it was unlawful to marry among the Canaanites. These unions were unlawful and considered fornication.

These are all forbidden sexual relationships. These unions are unlawful with no legal validity in the eyes of Adonai. They are not recognized as established unions. They hold no legal status from the onset. Asking Adonai to bless these unions would be akin to petitioning a court for permits to open a meth lab, or suing the owner of a meth lab for not honoring vacation days as agreed upon when the worker was hired to illegally make and distribute methamphetamines.

When Yeshua teaches that it is permitted to only "put away" (and not provide a writ) the forbidden partner in the case of fornication, the reason is that there was no legitimate marriage to void in the first place! Adonai does not require a writ to sever such a union. Requiring a legal divorce would be akin to His acknowledging the forbidden union, which He will not do.

Let's insert the definitions:

> It hath been said, Whosoever shall separate from his wife, let him give her a lawful divorce. But I say unto you, that whosoever separates from his wife, (saving for the cause of an unrecognized marriage which would require no divorce), causes her to commit adultery: and whosoever shall marry her who is only separated from her husband commits adultery. (Matt 5:31-32)

Yeshua's rendering of the matter is completely consistent with His Father's.

4

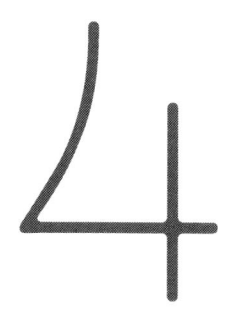

CONTEXT, CONTEXT, CONTEXT!

Why did God angrily say that He "hated divorce" in Malachi 2?

He didn't.

He said that He hated "putting away," a separation without a writ, "Because you have not kept My ways, but have shown partiality in the instruction" (Malachi 2:9). Again, these men were only doing part of the procedure and not providing the women the freedom to remarry.

Here is the passage with added clarity in light of the context....

> Judah hath dealt treacherously, and an abomination is committed in Israel and in Jerusalem; for Judah hath profaned the holiness of the LORD which he loved, and hath married the daughter of a strange god...Yet ye say, Wherefore? Because the LORD hath been witness between thee and the wife of thy youth, against whom thou hast dealt treacherously: yet [is] she thy companion, and the wife of thy covenant.

> And did not he make one? Yet had he the residue of the spirit. And wherefore one? That he might seek a godly seed. Therefore take heed to your spirit, and let none deal treacherously against the wife of his youth. For the LORD, the God of Israel, saith that he hateth putting away (shalach: separating without a writ): for [one] covereth violence with his garment, saith the LORD of hosts: therefore take heed to your spirit, that ye deal not treacherously. (Malachi 2:11-16).

Because these men had remarried illegally, separating from their wives without giving them a Certificate of Divorce, they were in adultery. Adonai clearly hates that!

Remarriage

Did Paul ban remarriage after divorce, contradicting the eternal word of Adonai, or is he sometimes misunderstood? Due to frequent misunderstandings of 1 Corinthians 7:10-11, it's been assumed that Paul forbade all remarriage when ironically, Paul did just the opposite.

> And unto the married...let not the wife depart (*chorizo*) from her husband; but and if she depart (*chorizo*), let her remain unmarried (*agamos*), or let her be reconciled to her husband; and let not the husband put away (*aphiemi*, "to dismiss") his wife. (1 Corinthians 7:10-11 KJV)

Picking up this ancient letter from the middle, reading it from a Western perspective and in another language, one might suspect that Paul is condemning divorce and remarriage. However, in verse 1, Paul is not speaking about divorce, nor does he use the word for divorce.

> Now concerning the things whereof ye wrote unto me: it is good for a man not to touch a woman. (1 Corinthians 7:1 KJV)

Paul is referring to something he had written to them beforehand about a man not touching a woman. The church at Corinth required an adjustment on something for Paul to take the trouble to write to them to correct it. The previously hedonistic Corinthians misunderstood Paul, and they even started separating perfectly healthy marriages as they leaned toward doctrines that were embedded in their worldview.

> Indeed Winter notes in "After Paul Left Corinth" that the slogan in question matches not with Gnosticism, but with a common aphorism used by those who reasoned 'on the grounds of first-century Platonic anthropology, philosophical hedonism, and social conventions' [p. 88] in which it was asserted that the body was designed for pleasure and that such activity did no harm to the soul. This was part of a secular more of ancient Corinth. (Winter, 2001)

The correction was due to the Corinthians' misunderstanding of what he was suggesting, not a sermon on divorce and remarriage. Paul discusses two issues that were prevailing issues at that time.

1. The "present distress" (see vs 26)
2. To be able to dedicate more fully to ministry during this present distress (see vs 32-35)

The danger that these people faced for their faith and mission was intense. Executions of entire families were not uncommon, so Paul's advice here is quite prudent. Just as it might be suggested to a husband and wife who were being deployed to Iraq in military service not to conceive a child in that circumstance, Paul was striving to reduce suffering, not rewriting the Torah from his own opinion. If a person could refrain from entering into a marital union in that situation, that would be advantageous.

Paul does, however, teach that those already married should not separate (see verse 5), and that if a single person cannot remain celibate, it is better to marry than to enter into forbidden sexual unions (see verses 7-9).

In this letter Paul does discuss divorce and remarriage. He references these marital statuses with the terms "bound" (legally married) and "loosed" (legally severed by spousal death or a legal divorce).

The word "unmarried" (*agamos*) is most often translated as the act of getting married, not "remaining married." Again, if the argument is that first marriages are *never severable*, then how can a woman argued to be *forever bound* to the first marriage remain "unmarried"? By definition of that argument, the point is that she can *never be unmarried again*.

Paul, the Torah scholar of scholars, knows that the Torah expressly and specifically forbids remarrying one's former spouse after a lawful divorce, so he would be loath to teach against it, as he continuously repeats his view of the Torah being holy and good.

> If a man marries a woman who becomes displeasing to him because he finds something indecent about her, and he writes her a certificate of divorce, gives it to her and sends her from his house, and if after she leaves his house she becomes the wife of another man, and her second husband dislikes her and writes her a certificate of divorce, gives it to her and sends her from his house, or if he dies, then her first husband, who divorced her, is not allowed to marry her again after she has been defiled. That would be detestable in the eyes of the Lord. Do not bring sin upon the land the Lord your God is giving you as an inheritance. (Deut. 24:1-4 NIV)

Later in this same chapter, Paul does deal with the question of divorce and remarriage. Paul uses the descriptive terms of marital status: "bound" and "loosed." To be bound by

Torah Law means to be married by contract; to be loosed means to be legally loosed from that contract (i.e., divorced or widowed).

> Art thou bound (by law) unto a wife? Seek not to be loosed (from the bonds of marriage). Art thou loosed from a wife? Seek not a wife. But and if thou marry, thou hast not sinned; and if a virgin marry, she hath not sinned. (1 Cor. 7:27- 28 KJV)

What could be simpler? In this present distress (see vs 26) do not get divorced. Paul instructs that If they are legally divorced or a widower, do not set out to find a new wife as this, for obvious reasons, is not a suitable time for betrothals. But, if those so desirous of companionship cannot function in the single life do get married, this is not sinful as legal marriage is a Torah-sanctioned act. Similarly, if a person who has never married (a virgin) opts to marry for the same reason, they have not sinned either.

Whom does he say has not sinned by marrying?

1. The one who is loosed (those divorced or widowed)

or

2. The virgin (those who have never been married at all)

Simply and plainly, Paul declares (as does Adonai) that remarriage after a divorce is not a sin. But wait...what about what Paul said to the Romans?

> The law hath dominion over a man as long as he liveth? For the woman which hath an husband is bound by the law to *her* husband so long as he liveth; but if the husband be dead, she is loosed from the law of *her* husband. So then if, while her husband liveth, she be married to another man, she shall be called an adulteress: but if her husband be dead, she is free from that

> law; so that she is no adulteress, though she be married to another man. (Romans 7:1-3 KJV)

There is a chapter break between chapters Six and Seven, so you might not notice the "break" in topic where Paul inexplicably starts discussing marriage. Paul is speaking of the wages of sin being death, etc, and suddenly he blurts out some sort of specification regarding marriage and divorce. It seems so out of place. Or does it?

Back up to Romans 7:1, and it identifies his audience.

> Know ye not, brethren, (for I speak to them that know the law,)...

"Them that know the law." Clearly this is a point he is making that can be only be understood by someone who has studied the Torah laws on marriage and divorce. Have you ever read Romans without meeting the criteria Paul set forth for reading it, which is knowing the Torah, and still thought you could understand and apply what he was saying?

What would you need to know about the law to understand what Paul is telling the Romans?

> For the woman which hath a husband is bound by the law to her husband so long as he liveth; but if the husband be dead, she is loosed from the law of her husband. So then if, while her husband liveth, she be married to another man, she shall be called an adulteress: but if her husband be dead, she is free from that law; so that she is no adulteress, though she be married to another man. (KJV)

Paul is discussing "the Law of the Husband," learned earlier in this booklet (Deut. 24).
What are the terms?

1. If the husband wants to divorce his wife, he must send her

away with a written bill of divorcement.
2. She is free to remarry.
3. If she does remarry and becomes divorced from her latter husband, the former husband may not remarry her.

Some who are not familiar with the Law of the Husband will interpret this to mean that people are released from the *whole law*. This has created a profound misunderstanding. However, when one learns this particular marital law, he or she may understand Paul's analogy and put together a wonderful mystery.

According to term #3 above, when a man and woman divorce, another contract between them is automatically created by the divorce, and that contract remains in effect for the duration of their lives. They are now automatically both bound to the *Law of the Husband*...which specifies that they may never remarry one other. Review Romans 7:1-2 with that new understanding:

> Know ye not, brethren, (for I speak to them that know the law,) the law hath dominion over a man as long as he liveth? (quoting Deut 24:3) For the woman which hath a husband is bound by the law to her husband so long as he liveth; but if the husband be dead, she is loosed from the law of her husband.

While the divorced couple is separated by certificate, the former husband and wife are also now bound by a contract that remains in effect even after the divorce, and that is that he may never remarry her. They are bound by the prohibition of ever reuniting according to the Torah marital law. This is clearly stated in the Law of the Husband. Even Adonai cannot remarry His beloved Israel whom He sent away and divorced. If He did so, He would be breaking His own law.

The writ of divorce stood against them.
Paul is bringing out something incredible that you *have to know Torah instruction* to understand and appreciate: there is *one way* by Torah law that *all* marital conditions are

completely voided and severed: IF THE HUSBAND DIES

This would, by extension, sever the PROHIBITION of remarrying the former spouse.

Paul mentions this not in the context of a discussion of whether or not divorce and remarriage is acknowledged by Adonai. The instruction on marriage and divorce was already established by Adonai and not questioned. Paul specifically addresses the prohibition clause in the "Law of the Husband" in regard to remarriage of His bride to HIM.

Jeremiah establishes that this was on the mind of Adonai when He promises to take Israel back and restore her.

> 'If a man divorces his wife and she leaves him and marries another man, should he return to her again? Would not the land be completely defiled? But you have lived as a prostitute with many lovers—would you now return to me?' declares the Lord. 'Look up to the barren heights and see. Is there any place where you have not been ravished? By the roadside you sat waiting for lovers, sat like a nomad in the desert. You have defiled the land with your prostitution and wickedness. Therefore the showers have been withheld, and no spring rains have fallen. Yet you have the brazen look of a prostitute; you refuse to blush with shame. Have you not just called to me: "'My Father, my friend from my youth.'" (Jer. 3:1-4 NIV)
>
> During the reign of King Josiah, the Lord said to me, 'Have you seen what faithless Israel has done? She has gone up on every high hill and under every spreading tree and has committed adultery there. I thought that after she had done all this she would return to me but she did not, and her unfaithful sister Judah saw it. I gave faithless Israel her certificate of divorce and sent her away

because of all her adulteries. Yet I saw that her unfaithful sister Judah had no fear; she also went out and committed adultery. Because Israel's immorality mattered so little to her, she defiled the land and committed adultery with stone and wood. In spite of all this, her unfaithful sister Judah did not return to me with all her heart, but only in pretense,' declares the Lord. The Lord said to me, 'Faithless Israel is more righteous than unfaithful Judah. Go, proclaim this message toward the north:

"'Return, faithless Israel,'" declares the Lord,

"'I will frown on you no longer,

for I am faithful,'" declares the Lord,

"'I will not be angry forever.

Only acknowledge your guilt—

you have rebelled against the Lord your God,

you have scattered your favors to foreign gods

under every spreading tree,

and have not obeyed me,'"

declares the Lord.

"'Return, faithless people,'" declares the Lord, "'for I am your husband. I will choose you—one from a town and two from a clan—and bring you to Zion. Then I will give you shepherds after my own heart, who will lead you with knowledge and understanding.'" (Jer. 3:6-15 NIV)

How can Adonai take back the bride He sent away and divorced without breaking His own law? This was the question of the ages. They first had to be released from the Law of the Husband. Divorce severs most of the connections, but it creates the connection of being forbidden to remarry one's former spouse.

> **Q.** What severs all marital connections?
> **A.** DEATH
>
> **Q.** What brings people BACK into covenant?
> **A.** BLOOD

The Bridegroom Yeshua dies, and all marital connections and prohibitions are PERMANENTLY loosed. He rises from the dead with a new/renewed covenant that Israel may enter into at THE WEDDING SUPPER OF THE LAMB

> Blessed are those who are invited to the wedding supper of the Lamb! (Rev. 19:9 NIV)

Have you ever wondered what the disciples meant by this question?

> Therefore, when they had come together, they asked Him, saying, 'Lord, will You at this time restore the kingdom to Israel?' (Acts 1:6 NKJV)

This is the question they were addressing: "When and how can the House of Israel come back like Adonai says will happen when Adonai's law says it can never happen?" Yeshua earlier had told his disciples:

> I was not sent except to the lost sheep of the house of Israel. (Matt. 15:24 NKJV)

Who is Israel?

Some may wonder, "But aren't Christians under the New

Covenant?" Let's return to the covenant foundation.

Q. To whom was the new covenant made?

A. "The days are coming, declares the Lord, when I will make a new covenant with the people of Israel and with the people of Judah." (Hebrews 8:8 NIV)

Hence, according to the Bible, those in the "New Covenant" are *either the people of Israel or the people of Judah*. In other words, if one is not a part of Israel, he or she is not a part of the New Covenant. If you are not a part of the New Covenant, you are not a part of Israel.

The death of the husband, which releases the bride from the law of the husband, and the resurrection of Him Who is the same today and forever automatically renews the covenant, for this is His Word and He IS His Word. *This is what the new covenant is.* It is not a new set of rules or vows. It is a new, sparkling clean exact copy of the same holiness He has always been, is now, and will ever be!

HE NEVER CHANGES!

The death and resurrection created a fresh new signature line where the bride can legitimately sign and be reunited with her groom.

Same Husband

Same Wife

Same covenant terms

But a renewed groom and a renewed bride

through DEATH and RESURRECTION

The writer to the Hebrews states:

> For if that first *had been faultless*, no cause have been sought for another. But God *found fault with them* and said: 'The days are coming, declares the Lord, when I will make a new covenant with the people of Israel and with the people of Judah.'
> (Hebrews 8:7-8)

This is the mystery of the gospel. The mystery of the gospel is not that "gentiles" are able to be grafted in after the cross. Being grafted into Israel was never a mystery. In fact, it was always the goal. Ruth, Rahab, and other converts were always welcomed in.

> For this reason, I, Paul, a prisoner for Christ Jesus on behalf of you Gentiles—assuming that you have heard of the stewardship of God's grace that was given to me for you, how the mystery was made known to me by revelation, as I have written briefly. When you read this, you can perceive my insight into the mystery of Christ, which was not made known to the sons of men in other generations as it has now been revealed to his holy apostles and prophets by the Spirit. This mystery is that the Gentiles are fellow heirs, members of the same body, and partakers of the promise in Christ Jesus through the gospel. (Eph. 3:1-6 ESV)

The alien joining Israel was never a mystery, nor is it a mystery among Jews today. People convert to Judaism all the time. Indeed, it was actually the point of having Israel as a formed nation...so one could leave the outside and come into the inside, so they could be set apart.

The "gentiles" here *include* the ones shunned by divorce and not eligible for remarriage until Yeshua died, rose with a new freshened covenant, and betrothed His bride. We need not bicker over senseless genealogies.

> But avoid foolish controversies and genealogies and arguments and quarrels about the law, because these are unprofitable and useless. (Titus 3:9 NIV)

If you weren't born into Judah, you may be a gentile (eligible for conversion), or you may be a gentile who is a descendent of the other tribes who were SHUNNED FOREVER due to the divorce writ and the list of covenant violations that *stood against them until it was nailed to the cross* at the crucifixion.

Let's read the Letter to the Colossians with trained eyes:

> For in Christ all the fullness of the Deity lives in bodily form, and in Christ you have been brought to fullness. He is the head over every power and authority. In him you were also circumcised with a circumcision not performed by human hands. Your whole self-ruled by the flesh was put off when you were circumcised by Christ, having been buried with him in baptism, in which you were also raised with him through your faith in the working of God, who raised him from the dead. When you were dead in your sins and in the uncircumcision of your flesh, God made you alive with Christ. He forgave us all our sins, having canceled the charge of our legal indebtedness, which stood against us and condemned us; he has taken it away, nailing it to the cross. And having disarmed the powers and authorities, he made a public spectacle of them, triumphing over them by the cross. (Col. 2:9-14 NIV)

This is the mysterious, secret pathway for even the unredeemable to be redeemed fully and restored back to the covenant...and all accomplished with **Him** keeping all of His perfect laws! What an intelligent Most High God we serve! Nothing is impossible with the Father, and it is all done by Him within His holy Law that holds the entire universe together.

Misunderstanding marital and divorce instruction results in pain, victimization, and bondage. Making an idol out of dysfunctional or abusive marriages to prove "spirituality" can cause believers to miss the greatest love story ever told! And WE are the love interest no less!

5

CONCLUSION

Not only did the Code of Hammurabi permit divorce and remarriage as the common law of the land that dominated Canaan, but so did Adonai's Law, which predates ALL other laws. The major discrepancy addressed was the legal process of attaining a legal divorce as a means to protect the right of women to live securely following a divorce.

Misunderstanding this topic has forced many pastors and churchgoers into terrible bondage. It has caused loneliness, pain, divisions, and broken hearts. But for anyone interested in the truth, you can trust that you have been released!

If you are a part of the "New Testament Church," you are declaring with joy that because of Messiah you are now fully restored to the Old Testament promises and the Old Testament instructions. You are *restored to* the Torah, *not delivered from* it.

The Torah has not been established by the Creator to show human beings how despicable they are, but to demonstrate through His outstretched hand how valuable each person is to Him. In Him, all things are possible, and even the unredeemable are shown, though His mercy, to be redeemed!

STUDY REVIEW QUESTIONS

1. What is a "writ" of divorce?

2. What is the difference between "divorce" and "put away"?

3. What are the terms of the Law of the Husband?

4. What is the main difference between the divorce procedures of the Code of Hammurabi and the Law of Adonai?

5. What did the Messiah promise He was not ever going to do in regards to the Law of Adonai?

6. Whom did Adonai divorce and why?

7. How can Adonai "remarry" Israel, whom He had divorced, without breaking the Law of the Husband?

8. What is the solution Adonai provided for broken marriage contracts?

9. What safeguards did Adonai build into Torah marital law to protect women?

10. What is the commission of Israel when it comes to the Nations?

APPENDIX A

Ancient Egyptian Divorce

In native Egyptian law, marriage was a private contract; there is no evidence that any civil or religious official participated. <u>No written document was required</u>. The marriage continued during mutual consent; either party could dissolve it at will, and we have no evidence that the law attached any penalty to divorce. Marriage could also be limited in advance to a definite period. (Chambliss, 1954, p. 62)

Divorce and remarriage were common in Egypt at all periods...The vocabulary for divorce, like that for marriage, reflected the fact that <u>marriage was, basically, living together; a man "left, abandoned" a woman; a woman "went (away from)" or "left, abandoned" a man</u>.

Although neither party had to provide legal (or social, moral or ethical) grounds for divorce, the economic responsibilities spelled out in the annuity contracts made this a serious step. Thus, normally a married woman was supported by her husband for as long as they remained married and his property was entailed for their children. Since even remarriage after the death of a first wife could lead to wrangling over property and inheritance rights, a bitter divorce and remarriage could lead to major legal contests.

If a man divorced his wife, he had to return her dowry (if she had brought one) and pay her a fine; if she divorced him, there was no fine. A spouse divorced for fault (including adultery) forfeited his or her share of the couple's joint property. After divorce, both were free to remarry. But it seems clear that, until the husband has returned his wife's dowry and paid her the fine, or until she has accepted it, the husband remained liable for supporting her, even if they were no longer living together. <u>Some (ex-)husbands, then as now, tried to avoid supporting their (ex-)wives</u>, and we have several references to a woman's biological family stepping in to support or assist her when her husband can't or won't. (Johnson, 2004)

APPENDIX B

Excerpts from the Code of Hammurabi (King, trans., 2008)

137. If a man wish to separate from a woman who has borne him children, or from his wife who has borne him children: then he shall give that wife her dowry, and a part of the usufruct of field, garden, and property, so that she can rear her children. When she has brought up her children, a portion of all that is given to the children, equal as that of one son, shall be given to her. She may then marry the man of her heart.

138. If a man wishes to separate from his wife who has borne him no children, he shall give her the amount of her purchase money and the dowry which she brought from her father's house, and let her go.

141. If a man's wife, who lives in his house, wishes to leave it, plunges into debt, tries to ruin her house, neglects her husband, and is judicially convicted: if her husband offer her release, she may go on her way, and he gives her nothing as a gift of release. If her husband does not wish to release her, and if he take another wife, she shall remain as servant in her husband's house.

142. If a woman quarrel with her husband, and say: "You are not congenial to me," the reasons for her prejudice must be presented. If she is guiltless, and <u>there is no fault on her part, but he leaves and neglects her</u>, then no guilt attaches to this woman, she shall take her dowry and go back to her father's house.

APPENDIX C

"Put Away and Divorce"
Mark 10:2 and Mark 10:4

2532 [e]	4334 [e]		5330 [e]
Kai	proselthontes		Pharisaioi
2 Καὶ	προσελθόντες	,	Φαρισαῖοι
And	having come to [him]		the Pharisees
Conj	V-APA-NMP		N-NMP

1905 [e]	846 [e]	1487 [e]
epērōtōn	auton	ei
ἐπηρώτων	αὐτὸν ,	εἰ
demanded	of him	if
V-IIA-3P	PPro-AM3S	Conj

1832 [e]	435 [e]	1135 [e]
exestin	andri	gynaika
ἔξεστιν	ἀνδρὶ	γυναῖκα
it is lawful	for a husband	a wife
V-PIA-3S	N-DMS	N-AFS

630 [e]	3985 [e]	846 [e]
apolysai	peirazontes	auton
ἀπολῦσαι ,	πειράζοντες	αὐτόν .
to divorce	testing	him
V-ANA	V-PPA-NMP	PPro-AM3S

	3588 [e]	1161 [e]	3004 [e]	2010 [e]
	hoi	de	eipan	Epetrepsen
4	οἱ	δὲ	εἶπαν ,	Ἐπέτρεψεν
	-	and	they said	permitted
	Art-NMP	Conj	V-AIA-3P	V-AIA-3S

3475 [e]	975 [e]	647 [e]
Mōusēs	biblion	apostasiou
Μωϋσῆς	βιβλίον	ἀποστασίου
Moses	a bill	of divorce
N-NMS	N-ANS	N-GNS

1125 [e]	2532 [e]	630 [e]
grapsai	kai	apolysai
γράψαι ,	καὶ	ἀπολῦσαι .
to write	and	to send [her] away
V-ANA	Conj	V-ANA

APPENDIX D

"Putting Away" (*apoluon*) Requires Divorce Certificate (*apostasion*)
Matthew 5:31-32

2046 [e]	1161 [e]	3739 [e]	302 [e]
Errethē	de	Hos	an
31 Ἐρρέθη	δέ ,	Ὃς	ἂν
It was said	also	whoever	anyhow
V-AIP-3S	Conj	RelPro-NMS	Prtcl

630 [e]	3588 [e]	1135 [e]
apolysē	tēn	gynaika
ἀπολύσῃ	τὴν	γυναῖκα
shall divorce	the	wife
V-ASA-3S	Art-AFS	N-AFS

846 [e]	1325 [e]	846 [e]	647 [e]
autou	dotō	autē	apostasion
αὐτοῦ ,	δότω	αὐτῇ	ἀποστάσιον :
of him	let him give	to her	a letter of divorce
PPro-GM3S	V-AMA-3S	PPro-DF3S	N-ANS

32 ἐγὼ δὲ λέγω ὑμῖν, ὅτι πᾶς ὁ ἀπολύων τὴν γυναῖκα αὐτοῦ, παρεκτὸς λόγου πορνείας, ποιεῖ

846 [e]	3431 [e]		2532 [e]
autēn	moicheuthēnai		kai
αὐτὴν	μοιχευθῆναι	;	καὶ
her	to commit adultery		and
PPro-AF3S	V-ANP		Conj

3739 [e]	1437 [e]	630 [e]
hos	ean	apolelymenēn
ὃς	ἐὰν	ἀπολελυμένην
whoever	if	her having been divorced
RelPro-NMS	Conj	V-RPM/P-AFS

1060 [e]		3429 [e]
gamēsē		moichatai
γαμήσῃ	,	μοιχᾶται .
shall marry		commits adultery
V-ASA-3S		V-PIM/P-3S

REFERENCES

Chambless, R. (1954). *Social thought: from Hammurabi to Comte.* New York: Dryden Press.

King, L. (trans.) (2008). The code of Hammurabi. New Haven, CT: Yale Law School. http://avalon.law.yale.edu/ancient/hamframe.asp. Retrieved 8/17/16.

Johnson, J. (2002). Women's legal rights in ancient Egypt. University of Chicago Library Digital collections. http://fathom.lib.uchicago.edu/1/777777190170/. Retrieved 8/17/16.

Kaiser, W. (1994). An introduction to biblical hermeneutics: the search for meaning. Grand Rapids: Zondervan.

King, L.W. (2014). *The code of Hammurabi.* North Charleston, SC: CreateSpace Independent Publishing Platform.

Winter, B. (2001). *When Paul Left Corinth: the influence of secular ethics and social change.* Grand Rapids, Michigan: Wm. B. Eerdmans Publishing Co.

ABOUT THE AUTHOR

Robin Gould, D.R.E., LMFT has a Master's Degree in Marriage & Family Therapy and a Doctorate in Religious Education. Practicing as a therapist since 2001, Dr. Gould specializes in Emotionally Focused Couple's Therapy and is currently conferencing on marital health. She is the author of several BEKY books in the BEKY Book series and hosts a radio show on Messianic Lamb Radio. She travels as a lecturer and public speaker enlightening Christians to the Messiah in the Old Testament, as well as emphasizing the relational aspects of the Torah to the Messianic Believer. The proud mother of two wonderful sons, she divides her time between Florida and Vermont with her husband, David. She may be contacted through her website: www.newcovenantpath.com

OTHER BOOKS BY THE AUTHOR

All titles are available on Amazon.

- *Colossal Controversies,* 2016
- *Divorce and Remarriage in the Bible,* 2016
- *Peter's Vision,* 2016
- *First Century Words Revealed to Twenty-First Century Believers,* 2017
- *The Forgiveness Tarts,* 2018

ACKNOWLEDGEMENTS

Thanks to Diane Schmid Laverty for her generous assistance in proofreading this booklet.

Thanks to Dr. Hollisa Alewine for her extensive contributions both in these pages as editor, and off these pages as an optimistic voice leading me to the paths of maturity and wisdom. Thank you for sharing your time and for investing in the community of women, helping their voices be heard for the Glory of the Kingdom. You are sincerely appreciated.

Thanks to Stephen E. Jones for his "nuts and bolts' study on this subject which inspired me to take this topic further and expand its focus. His work on this issue was instrumental in paving the way for me to connect the dots of grace.